Boyzone

in words and pictures

Richard Topping

|| •PARRAGON• ||

First published in 1999 by
Parragon
Queen Street House
4 Queen Street
Bath
BA1 1HE

Copyright © 1999 Parragon

Produced by Blackjacks

All rights reserved. No part of this publication
may be reproduced, stored in a retrieval
system, or transmitted by any means,
electronic, mechanical, photocopying,
recording or otherwise, without the prior
permission of the copyright holder.

British Library Cataloguing-in-Publication Data

A catalogue record for this book is available
from the British Library.

ISBN 0 75253 341 X

Printed in Italy

Contents

In the Beginning

Nowadays, you can't turn on the television or listen to the radio without being bombarded by the latest song from the latest boy band. But not all boy bands are the same, and the success enjoyed by many of today's newcomers owes a lot to the trail blazed by five ambitious and talented lads from Dublin.

In the early 1990s, its was American group New Kids on The Block and their English successors Take That who started the boy band phenomena that went on to sweep the world. But in 1993 Irish music agent Louis Walsh realised there was plenty of room at the top for the right kind of talent. Given Ireland's track record in spawning some of the best musicians of their generation – from the Boomtown Rats and Sinead O'Connor to U2 and The Cranberries – Walsh figured if you wanted to create a successful band, you couldn't choose a better place to do it than the Emerald Isle.

So he placed an advert in a Dublin newspaper, and found himself swamped by over 300 hopefuls, all dreaming of pop stardom. After a gruelling round of auditions and interviews he came up with the five best looking, best singing and best dancing boys of the bunch: Ronan Keating,

Stephen Gately, Mikey Graham, Keith Duffy and Shane Lynch. Five lads that went on to become Boyzone.

Unknowingly Walsh had stumbled onto something else. Despite coming from different backgrounds in the Northside of Dublin, the boys bonded immediately. Whereas many of today's boy bands look and sound really 'manufactured' there was a chemistry with Boyzone that was to help make them one of the most successful Irish bands of all time.

The lads worked hard rehearsing songs and learning dance routines, and after six months of exhausting preparation, they were ready to be launched!

In May 1994 they released their first single – 'Working My Way Back To You' – which was a cover of an old Detroit Spinners song. It went straight to No. 3 in the Irish charts and set them up for their next big hit, 'Love Me For a Reason', a cover of an Osmonds track. This was the song that put them on the map, reaching No.1 in Ireland and No.2 in the UK, selling an amazing 600,000 copies.

Boyzone had arrived!

Although Boyzone doesn't have a 'lead singer' as such, it's definitely Ronan Keating who's grown to become the main front-man – despite being 'the baby' of the band (he was only sixteen when the band got together!). His main ambition is to be a big singer/songwriter like George Michael, and with the success of Boyzone, it's hard not to see that happening.

"I wouldn't do anything differently," says Ronan of his rapid rise to fame "We've made mistakes but they've brought us to where we are, so I won't change a thing."

For Ronan it's the fans that make it all worthwhile. "The best thing is how genuine they are to us – they'd never treat us badly. If they didn't respect us, it'd be hard to carry on and enjoy it, but they do have respect. They understand when we want to be left alone."

Ronan copes with the pressures of fame by being as professional as possible. "I guess I stay really focused. It's not like I get up in the morning and think, 'right I have to be like this today'. It's a train of thought I'm always in. I guess I'm the type of person you have to be to get through it."

KEEPING IT GOING

All too often boy bands disappear as swiftly as they appear. The reason is usually because they simply don't have the song writing skills to sustain a credible career.

In 1995, the lads decided they were going to take a risk by releasing their own song. The big cheeses at the record company weren't too pleased, because they figured the band could risk everything they'd achieved so far by releasing a duff single - especially one that was going to be crucial to the launch of their album! But the song - 'Key to My Life' written by Ronan, Steve and Mikey - was already a big hit in the live gigs and the boys weren't going to be put off.

The boys' faith in themselves paid off. 'Key to My Life' went to number 3 in the UK charts, and suddenly marked them out as a serious band. While their rivals Take That were still riding high in the charts, it was obvious that a new force had entered the boy band arena. Boyzone were here to stay.

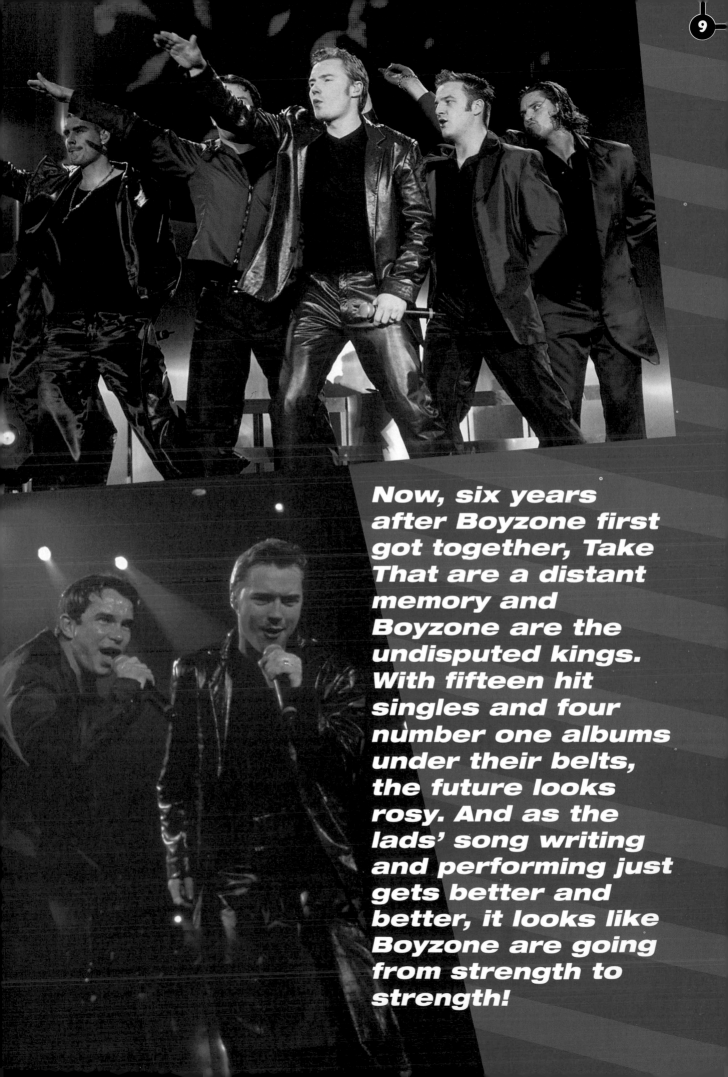

Now, six years after Boyzone first got together, Take That are a distant memory and Boyzone are the undisputed kings. With fifteen hit singles and four number one albums under their belts, the future looks rosy. And as the lads' song writing and performing just gets better and better, it looks like Boyzone are going from strength to strength!

Shane Lynch always wanted to be a pop star, and from the age of 12 he was already planning how he could make it into the big time. It took him a while to realise his ambition, but even while Boyzone was taking off, he continued working for his Dad at a garage in Dublin and never once forgot his roots.

"I want to prove that a normal Joe Soap who was a mechanic can do something with his life. I want to be able to turn around to my kids one day and say 'your Dad was a mechanic and look what he became just by being in the right place at the right time'."

But despite the band's success, Shane's very matter of fact about the way things could have turned out. "The whole thing has been a complete bonus, we didn't expect any of this, we didn't know it was gonna go anywhere."

Funnily enough, the first time Shane realised he was famous was not at one of his own gigs, but when he went to see arch-rivals Take That playing in Dublin. "I'd been in the paper the day or the week before, and while I was at the concert loads of people asked me for me autograph. It was before we'd even put out a record. I thought I was the business!"

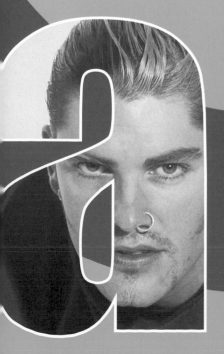

FACT FILE

Name: Shane Eamon Mark Stephen Lynch

Birthday: 3rd July 1976

Starsign: Cancer

Height: 6'

Shoe size: 9

Eyes: Blue

Family: Five sisters (Tara & Alison, older, twins Keavy and Edele and Naomi, all younger)

FACT FILE

Name: Ronan Patrick John Keating

Birthday: 3rd March 1977

Starsign: Pisces

Height: 5' 9"

Shoe size: 9

Eyes: Blue

Family: Three brothers (Ciaran, Gerard and Gary, all older), one sister – Linda (older). Two nephews (Conal and Rory)

the fame

How do the boys cope with being famous?
Pretty well by all accounts. They all come from
good solid families and it's the love of those close
to them that keeps their feet on the ground.

game

"My friends are very important to me, the friends that have been there since I was fifteen or sixteen. They are my best buddies now and they're not taken away by this band thing at all." - Keith

"The best thing about being in Boyzone is being in Boyzone! Singing and writing songs is all I ever wanted. It's a dream come true." — Ronan

"It's the feeling that all eyes are looking at you. I don't think I'll ever get used to being stared at." - Mikey

Mikey Grahams's the oldest of the lads, beating Keith by a good two years! Before he was plucked from the hundreds of hopefuls, he'd had quite a few jobs – a milkman, barman, supermarket shop assistant, department store porter and, just like Shane, a motor mechanic.

Mike's the big thinker in the band and probably worries about things more than the rest. "We've all got ideas about how the band will change, but I'm not sure that my thoughts are best... and I'm not exactly sure anyone would listen to me anyway!" Despite his modesty, Mike's much respected by the other lads. "He's quite sensible in the sense that he likes to think about things and make sure everything's alright," says Shane.

Even so, Mike's proud of his place in Ireland's hottest musical act. "This is my job, I do it well and I get paid good!"

KEV

relatio

Romance is never easy when you're in a band idolised by women the world over, constantly travelling the globe promoting your records. But the Boyzone lads have worked hard at their relationships.

"Yvonne (Ronan's wife) has been a tower of strength to me since Mam died. She's been there for me through it all. She has been my best friend. I don't know what I would have done without her and my family" – Ronan

"The test of mine and Lisa's love is that we've always worked our problems out and we're still together. Lisa and my family and mates have really stuck by me through all the madness that goes with Boyzone." – Keith

"People always had partners, now we've decided to be open about it. We're human beings. You can't shelter yourself from life, and the fans understand that. Thankfully, they see us as normal people" – Steve

nships

FACT FILE

Name: Michael Christopher Charles Graham

Birthday: 15th August 1972

Starsign: Leo

Height: 5'8"

Shoe size: 8

Eyes: Blue

Family: One brother (Niall, older) five sisters (Yvonne, Avril, Catherine, twins Clare and Deborah, all older). A daughter called Hannah.

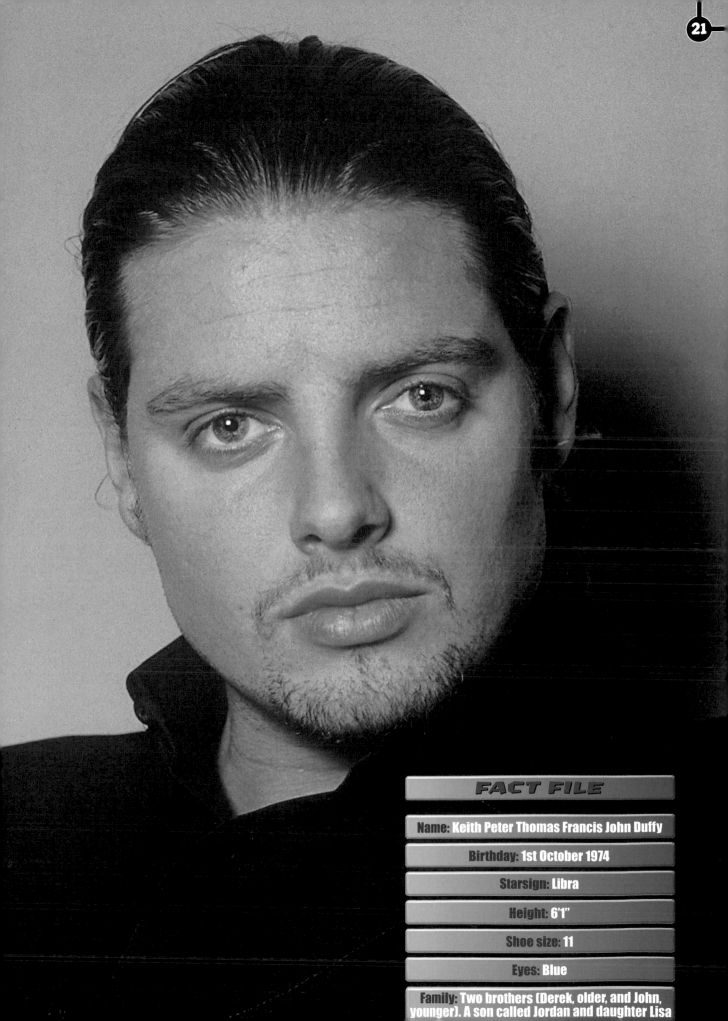

FACT FILE

Name: Keith Peter Thomas Francis John Duffy

Birthday: 1st October 1974

Starsign: Libra

Height: 6'1"

Shoe size: 11

Eyes: Blue

Family: Two brothers (Derek, older, and John, younger). A son called Jordan and daughter Lisa

KG

23

Keith Duffy's the second oldest of the lads, and has hidden talents as a drummer. Before Boyzone he used to play drums for a local band called The Burning Effigy and also for a cover band called Toledo Moon.

Keith's got a lot of drive to succeed, "I'm more ambitious than ever. If you lose your ambition there's no point in staying in the business." But like all of the band members, he's very practical about his success "Fame never really gave me a buzz, to be honest. I never really looked at myself as a famous person, just an ordinary bloke from Dublin. We just do a job and do it as well as we can."

Playing live is what gives Keith his best thrills. "My favourite bit is being up on stage performing. You get appreciation from the crowd and it makes you feel like a wonderful person."

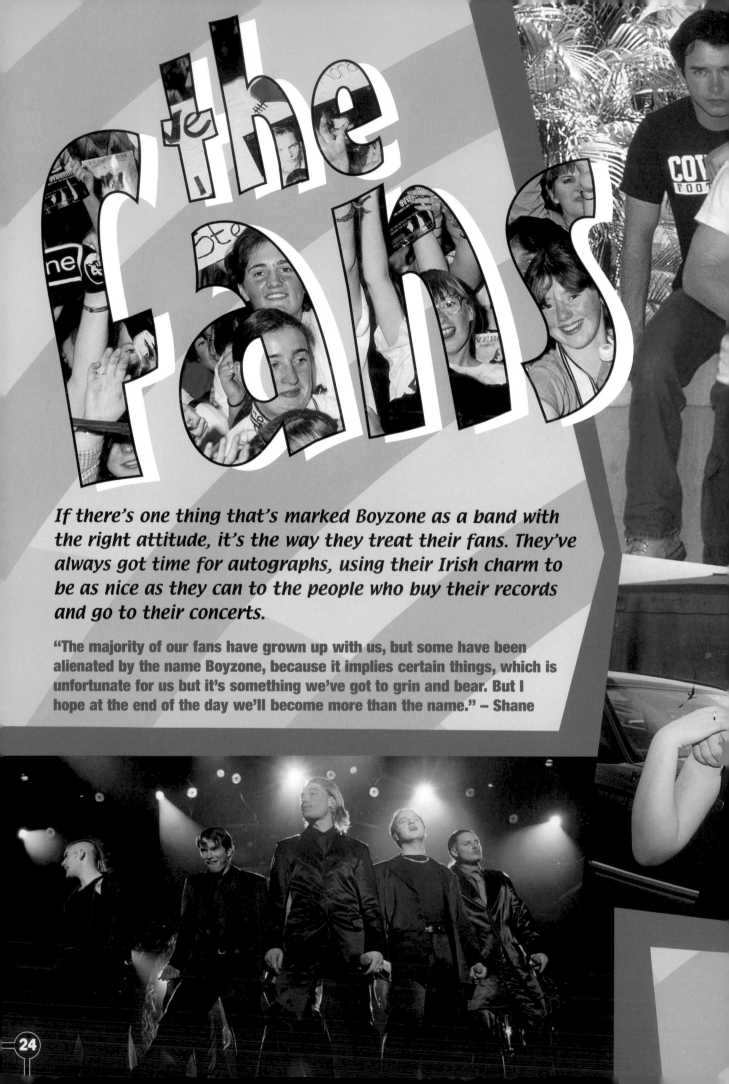

the fans

If there's one thing that's marked Boyzone as a band with the right attitude, it's the way they treat their fans. They've always got time for autographs, using their Irish charm to be as nice as they can to the people who buy their records and go to their concerts.

"The majority of our fans have grown up with us, but some have been alienated by the name Boyzone, because it implies certain things, which is unfortunate for us but it's something we've got to grin and bear. But I hope at the end of the day we'll become more than the name." – Shane

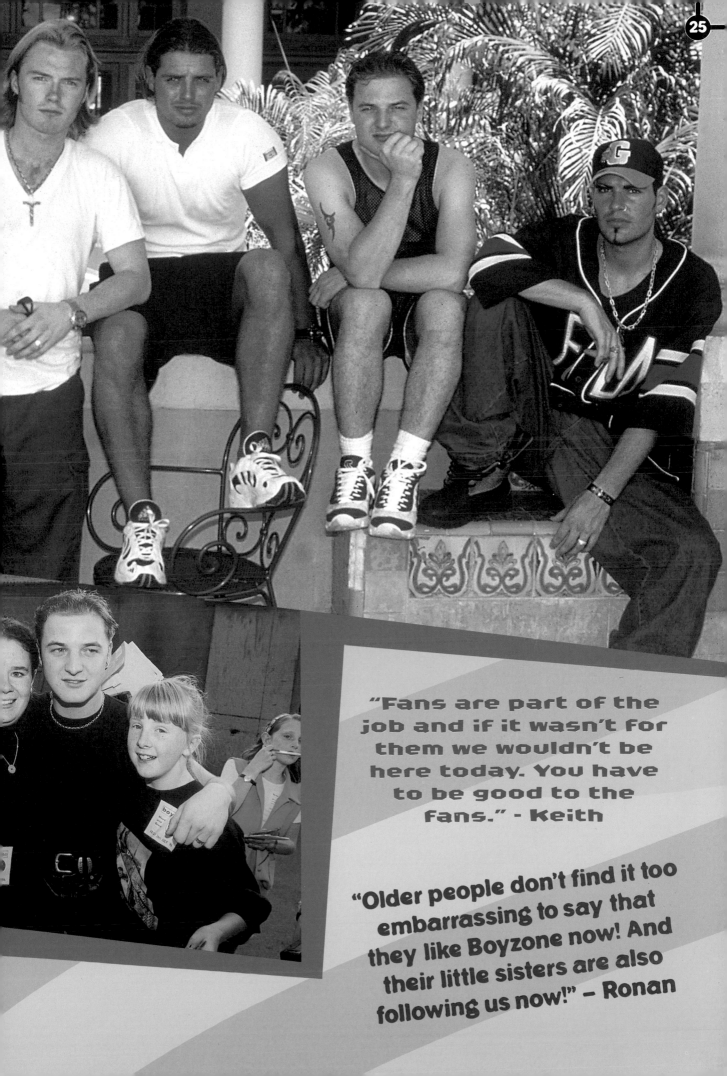

"Fans are part of the job and if it wasn't for them we wouldn't be here today. You have to be good to the fans." - Keith

"Older people don't find it too embarrassing to say that they like Boyzone now! And their little sisters are also following us now!" – Ronan

St

Stephen Gately's connections with the Irish music scene go back a long way, when he got a cameo role at the beginning of *The Commitments*, a film about a young Irish band trying to hit the bigtime!

As someone who'd been acting and modelling since the age of 16, Stephen looked certain to succeed, whatever he did. "I remember saying to two of my classmates at school, 'In a few years my autograph will be worth something'."

But despite his fame, Stephen's still a family man and likes nothing better than to hang out with his young nephews Jordan and Brendan. "I spend a lot of time with them because I want them to know who I am. I love my time with them. It's family stuff... more important than anything I do."

eve

FACT FILE

Name: Stephen Patrick David Gately

Birthday: 17th March 1976

Starsign: Pisces

Height: 5'7"

Shoe size: 7

Eyes: Blue

Family: Three brothers (Mark & Alan, both older, and Tony, younger), one sister (Michelle, older). Two nephews (Brandon and Jordan).

Singles

Title	Highest UK Chart Position
Love Me For A Reason	2
Key To My Life	3
So Good	3
Father And Son	2
Coming Home Now	4
Words	1
A Different Beat	1
Isn't It A Wonder	2
Picture Of You	2
Baby Can I Hold You	2
All That I Need	1
No Matter What	1
I Love The Way You Love Me	2
When The Going Gets Tough	1
You Needed Me	1

Albums

Title	Highest UK Chart Position
Said And Done	1
A Different Beat	1
Where We Belong	1
By Request	1

The Secret of Boyzone

"If I knew that, I'd be selling it! Staying grounded is a good answer. We've travelled the world six times, we've performed in prestigious venues and we've made a lot of money. We've done very well for ourselves, but as people, we're still the same. What people find very hard in this business is being nice, but it's not a chore for us, cos we are nice."
Ronan Keating